Dedicated to Lucienne

Table of Contents

THE **Slip** & **Fall** **Prevention** HANDBOOK

You Make the Difference

By an **Orthopedic Surgeon**

M. E. Hecht, M.D.

INTRODUCTION

There are some words that ring with truth. No matter the age, the language, the surround, the source - they ring with truth.

We all know them, we all know to act on them, but we sometimes overlook or disregard them at our own cost.

They are simply these –

"<u>You</u> Make the Difference".

If this book serves no other purpose than to call out the words "YOU MAKE THE DIFFERENCE", it will have reached its goal in Slip and Fall Prevention.

Most injuries happen in the place we feel the most secure-HOME. But our haven in this wide-world, the place in which we feel most secure, can be full of hazards - dangerous just because it's familiar and of its everyday character.

Statistics tell us that over 70% of fractures in those over 55 years of age - happen if not within the home then within yards of it. These injuries can be anything from a fracture of the wrist, requiring only a cast for a few weeks, to a life threatening hip fracture requiring surgery, hospitalization, and weeks of rehabilitation, even ending in a permanent assisted living facility. The least you may get by with is a sprain, or being black and blue from top-to-bottom. None of which desirable!

Consider, how often you've heard from someone who you had to accompany to the emergency room for a broken wrist, or someone to whose bedside you've come to (after a Slip and Fall accident). "I was simply at home getting ready to…..". Or I just tripped over the rug in my hallway", or even "the lights weren't on, so I didn't see..." Sound familiar?

Some fractures occur as we grow a bit older because our eyesight, attention and coordination aren't quite what they used to be. But just as many, because your home wasn't what I call, "Slip and Fall proofed."

Much of what you will find in this book is COMMON SENSE. Many of these things you may have thought about and even set up for yourself. But, perhaps, there are some hazards you haven't thought of, or again perhaps there's a new preventative measure you can initiate. What I hope to do, above anything else is to present the problem in a comprehensive, organized, and how-to-format.

Then too, this book is also meant as a handbook or an interactive manual to help you prevent accidents. It will take you through a step-by-step, area-by-area, and even site-by-site practical plan. It will ask you to fill out pertinent lists and questions, what you have done about them - in a word - to be proactive on your own behalf!

It will offer you, and your near and dear a checklist of hazards to be neutralized so as not to Slip and Fall. It will help you to control, and yes, manage your immediate environment. And I hope as you use the book you will find yourself, more and more sure that you _have_ been active and effective on behalf of your own safety.

If I were to suggest another mantra for this book it would be: **ANTICIPATE, ORGANIZE and AVOID**. These words will underlie each chapter of this book. And having said that, I reiterate that when push comes to shove, an informed and prepared <u>You</u> is still the most important prevention against Slip and Falls.

Armed with these suggestions, I hope you will begin to use, benefit from, and reuse the Slip and Fall Prevention Handbook.

How to use AND Reuse this Handbook

There is such a quantity of information in this book, that you may find that one reading is not sufficient to digest and retain it all. I suggest that you not worry if you fail on first sight to recall all the information presented in a chapter or section. Feel free to use and <u>reuse</u> the book to your benefit. And give attention to those parts that are particularly helpful to you. If you use and re-use, you won't need to rely on memory. And I won't even begin to comment on short term memory blanks in the over sixty crowd.

At the end of each chapter you will find check-off lists and notes. Once you've read the chapter, individualize, or add thoughts relevant to your own domicile and needs, and record them.

You may also find this a place to record critical names, numbers, and addresses. So as you use the information in this book be sure to have a pen or pencil handy. **Remember "You" are your most important prevention against Slip and Fall!** Therefore, make use of everything including these lists.

Lastly, I cannot think of a better reaction, than if you come to the journal at the end of each chapter, and are able to note...aha!... but she forgot <u>this one</u>! By all means...add away!

"Slow but steady wins the race".

- Aesop

Cause of Falls

Falls are often spoken of as 'accidents'. However falls are rarely completely accidental. This means that they don't just happen. There is a reason why a person falls.

OBSERVATION

The more risks a person encounters, the more likely they are to fall.

Therefore, the more things you can do to eliminate or reduce risks, the better.

Often it's the outcome of circumstances or events where a number of risk factors combine and interact. But many of these can be avoided.

Falling is not an inevitable part of aging, nor are falls simply caused by unavoidable objects or surroundings.

We need to step back and look at the big 'cause' picture.

The 5 Factors

1. **Impaired Vision**: poor eyesight, poor hearing, or both.

2. **Medications**: medication and side-effects.

3. **Activity:** muscle weakness, lack of exercise, or activity.

4. **Health Factors**: nutrition, healthy living habits.

5. **Environment:** Home Safety Hazards in-and-around the home and in public places.

11

 **VISION**

If you don't see it, you can't avoid it - anything from a curb to your pet.

You Make the Difference

Clean your glasses daily. Be careful of bifocals when negotiating steps or stairs. Having two pairs of glasses may be safer than bifocals - one for reading and one for long distance. Also have glasses consistently at a location easy to find.

▪ Check your vision regularly with your oculist or optometrist - your vision may change with passing years.

▪ Good lighting throughout the home helps - use 75W + bulbs.

▪ Wear a hat or sunglasses when outside to reduce the effects of glare.

▪ Consider contrast markings on the edge of steps or stairs.

▪ Use night lights /or have a small flashlight at hand when moving around your home at night.

 HEARING

Trust your hearing to help ID approaching trouble even if you don't yet see it.

12

You Make the Difference
Approaching cars or equipment is generally heard before seen. Have your hearing checked every year or two. If you need a hearing aid, don't be vain, use one!

- Be aware that in a crowded or noisy situation, hearing may be only so-so.

- Except in freezing weather, consider driving with the window at least partially down the better to hear approaching cars etc.

- If you fail to understand words spoken to you, don't hesitate to ask someone who may have better hearing, what was said, or to repeat the response. This is especially important, if your MD is talking.

 MEDICATIONS
As we age, we may need to increase or change our medications. And - their effect may change also.

You Make the Difference
Check with your MD - even reminding him if necessary of what you're using. Our reactions to medications do change - we may become more or less sensitive to them, needing greater or lesser doses, we may develop adverse reactions to them, or we may need to cease taking some altogether.

- Check with your MD - Meds may begin to produce side effects with <u>continued use</u> (e.g. dizziness, confusion, drowsiness, difficulty balancing, and blurred vision). I don't think I need belabor the point.

- Record your list of Meds regularly taken, and ask your pharmacist or MD about the side effects of each medication you take. And what, if any are the cross reactions!

- Again, remind your MD of your entire list of medications, so that he may modify them if needed in response to your reaction to them. For example there are many kinds of pain Meds; one may have become ineffective, another may begin to cause GI problems, and so on. There are almost always choices which can tailor your Meds to you as an individual. But if you don't give feedback to those who can adjust them, you are contributing to the problem.

- Check all Meds to be sure they have not passed expiration dates. And know what effect alcohol intake has on them.

- Last but perhaps not least, a list of common side effects is included in every new or renewed prescription. Granted they come with reams of technical or "scientific" information which may not mean much to you, and granted they are printed in a 'Fly-Speck' type size. However either have someone who can read them to you, or try your handy magnifying glass.

ACTIVITY

A certain amount of muscle loss, balance and flexibility accompanies aging.

You Make the Difference

Physical activity and exercise helps preserve what we have. You've heard this one from a hundred different sources "you must exercise", and you know you must heed the advice. What is sometimes forgotten with this advice is that you may have some degree of Arthritis (also a very common happening as we age), and so exercise may evoke pain.

Many of us find this unhappy concurrence. BUT doing nothing at all about it is even more unhappy making and even more contributive to its progression.

*Near the end of this book you will find in Chapter 9 suggested age modified exercises. Simple, easy to do and I hope diverting.

HEALTH FACTORS

A healthy diet and fluid intake helps maintain energy and the body's muscle tone.

You Make the Difference

There are reams of material written on healthy diet and exercise. Most of them are effective and do-able. You want to be sure that the ones you are using are age pertinent, and modified to your individual needs. Again a quick call to your MD will guide you.

I always warn my patients against one-note or 'curative' diets, the grapefruit- and-nothing- else-for-a -week type. Generally speaking they're not the wisest for those of us over 60.

- Balanced diet and nutritional suggestions are available at your doctor's office. Take one of the informational pamphlets on the subject and follow as much as possible, after consult with your MD.

- With regard to bone fractures, a daily calcium intake of 1000 – 1500mg. and 60 units of Vitamin D is advisable. This equates to 4 servings of dairy food per day. One serving is a glass of milk, a small tub of yogurt or a slice of cheese. For those who are lactose intolerant try calcium fortified soy milk. All this tends to help maintain the health of bones increasingly frail or under calcified as we age. I don't subscribe to any of the 'bone-sparing' Meds, neither the injectable nor the oral anti-osteoporotics. There's a good deal of evidence they don't prevent fractures, and a good deal of evidence of undesirable side effects.

- See your dentist on a regular schedule, so teeth problems never interfere with healthy food intake.

- See your medical doctor so physical changes or developments can be adjusted by him to your maximum benefit. Again, on each visit go through your list of Meds and dietary supplements (vitamins, minerals, etc.)

- The person who noted "you are what you eat," was not far off the mark. You may have a friendly local dietician or nutritionist-by all means take advantage of same.

 **ENVIRONMENT**

Most injuries happen where we feel most secure-HOME.

You Make the Difference

Much of this book deals specifically with how to avoid Slip and Fall trouble in your own the home, and when you venture abroad – in your immediate 'environment'. Statistics have been published based on reported actuarial records. I think you will find them interesting.

- **Some Where's**
  - ✓ Between 60 and 65 percent of falls happen at home.
  - ✓ Nearly 20 percent happen in medical or nursing facilities.
  - ✓ The remaining are scattered in location (Public facility's and recreational areas.)

- **Some When's**
  - ✓ Peak hours 9am to 5PM.
  - ✓ No significant seasonal element.
  - ✓ Weekdays more than weekends (???! but true.)

- **Some Who's**
  - ✓ Women more frequently than men.

✓ Mortality subsequent to fall increases significantly with age (especially over 75yrs.)

- **Some Why's**
  ✓ Trip on carpet, slip in bathroom and/or shower.
  ✓ Loss of balance (especially immediately on rising from chair or bed.)
  ✓ While dressing.
  ✓ Loss of balance walking in house.
  ✓ Backwards fall from walker.

Knowing some of these may give some food for thought.

JOURNAL

_____

_____

_____

_____

_____

_____

_____

_____

_____

_____

_____

_____

_____

CHAPTER 1
COMMON FRACTURE TYPES

- Injuries at or near the home and what they mean
- Common Fractures Types

Injuries at or Near Home and What they Mean

When we speak of Slips and Falls we should know what they involve in terms of consequence. About one third of the elder population over the age of 65 falls each year, and the risk of falls increases proportionately with age. At 80 years, over half of seniors fall annually.

As alarming as these stats are, these documented statistics fall short of the actual number since many incidents are unreported by seniors, and unrecognized by family members or caregivers.

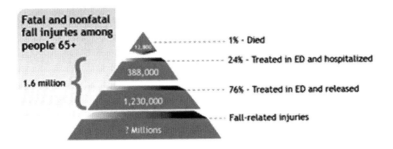

Fatal and nonfatal fall injuries among people 65+

1.6 million

43,800
388,000
1,230,000
? Millions

1% - Died
24% - Treated in ED and hospitalized
76% - Treated in ED and released
Fall-related injuries

One of the most serious and unfortunately common is that of the fracture, breaking a bone, or even bones.

So here are the garden varieties that are reported. Many of them you will have heard of, or may have happened to someone you know.

Common Fracture Types

The Wrist Fracture (often called a Colles fracture)
Once we know we are falling we tend to use an outstretched hand to break-the-fall. As we reach out with our arm to brace against the fall, its impact is visited on the ends of the radius and the ulna, or in plain terms the 'wrist.' It is not the most serious of fractures, but it is both painful and disabling, if it happens to your dominant hand.

Wrist Fracture Treatment

Traditional treatment consists of a manipulation to get the bones back as close as possible to anatomic normality. Then a short arm cast is applied (from knuckles to elbow).

A wrist fracture may also be operated on under regional anesthesia, the pieces 'reduced', or put back in place as close as possible, and then pinned either internally or with an external fixator.

These fractures have a high rate of healing, with either method. Usually the wrist is restored to useful function but rarely entirely that of pre-fracture movement. It can leave some stiffness and limitation of the wrist. These can and should be improved with the post injury Physical Therapy.

Healing: Estimated healing time 4-6 weeks.

The Shoulder Fracture

Such a fall may produce a fracture of the upper part of your arm or (humerus). It can break in one or several pieces. This fracture may result in noticeable stiffness and diminished range of shoulder motion.

Shoulder Fracture Treatment

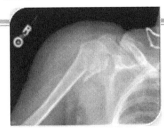

The Shoulder Fracture treatment is usually just a sling followed with physical therapy as soon as tolerated to restore motion. Interestingly, these fractures tend to heal somewhat faster than the wrist. Early gentle range of motion may be attempted - always remember that the severity and complexity of the fracture will dictate when motion can begin. Internal fixation maybe used for severely displaced fractures.

Healing: Estimated healing time 3-6 weeks.

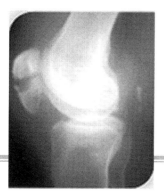

The Fracture of the Patella
(Knee cap)

This fracture is common after when one falls directly on one's knees. The knee cap can break in two or several pieces.

Knee Cap Fracture Treatment

The Fractures of the patella are generally operated and fixed internally with pins or screws. If good stability of the bones are achieved, a soft cast may be used with a simple splint and no further need of a plaster cast. Limited range of motion is started very early if the fixation is stable and near anatomic.

Healing: Estimated healing time 6-8 weeks.

The Ankle Fracture
This fracture may also happen especially if a slip is involved. These fractures range from the simple and relatively minor to a disabling injury, that may lead to arthritis, permanent stiffness and pain. It may consist of the fracture of one ankle bone with a simple, single break, even not displaced, or on the other hand, involve severe consequences to all three bones of the ankle.

Ankle Fracture Treatment

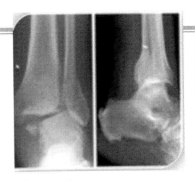

The ankle fracture treatment depends entirely upon the nature of the fracture. For the simple fracture there is a choice as to whether to use a cast, fix it internally, or even with an external fixator.

The advantage of internal fixation if successful (firm and anatomic reduction) is that it allows for early range of motion of the joint. This is less true of the external fixator, and less range of motion is possible. In general, casts for the older patient may not be the way to go early, as range of motion is key to the successful outcome.

Healing: Estimated healing time 6 -12 weeks

The Hip Fracture

These are really to be prevented at all costs. They are not infrequently life threatening, and/or permanently disabling.

There are basically two types of hip fracture: at the neck of the femur, or Intertrochanteric area.

24

Hip Fracture Treatment

The femoral neck fracture occurs near the head of the femur. In its most severe form, circulation to the head is disrupted. It is treated with either simple nailing in place, or in the disrupted type, with a hip replacement.

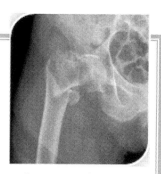

**Intertrochanteric Fracture: This fracture occurs lower down the femur and is almost invariably treated surgically with open surgical reduction and fixation. As contradictory as it may sound the conservative treatment for these fractures is surgery!

Healing: Estimated healing time 12 -16 weeks depending on the type, location, displacement and severity.

Historically these fractures were treated either with a body cast or traction with bed rest. Either method involved weeks, even months, of traction with either bed rest or complete inactivity. The problem here was that this treatment encouraged permanent stiffness, inaccurate reduction, atrophy of all leg muscles, sub-optimal deep breathing, even pneumonia, diminished circulation of the affected leg, and possible encouragement of dangerous clot formation.

I think it is easy to understand how the mortality rate from these fractures dropped dramatically, when we were able to fix the fracture internally and get the patient up and moving <u>within days</u> - Even though it meant major surgery.

Here is a happy thought - most of these fractures, especially in women are neck fractures. Many are associated with osteoarthritis and osteoporosis, so that the surgeon may opt to replace the hip with a total hip prosthesis. Thus converting a negative experience (the fracture) into a painless functioning joint giving the ability to stand and walk within days.

Hip! Hip! Hooray!

JOURNAL

CHAPTER 2
THE MORAL OF THE STORY

2

The Moral of the Story

As an older person, you may no longer assume that hazards don't lie within the familiar; within your home, your safe and sound area.

Think about how often you've heard from someone who was injured in their own house, or on their own front porch, say something like this..."I don't understand, I was just walking into my hallway or was just crossing to my door when.....boom!"

The Moral of the Story:

- **Anticipate.** If you're ready to go somewhere or do something, particularly if it is not familiar, think about what can be difficult, or problematic. Think before you leap, or even hop!

- **Use your brain at all times.** Don't do anything on automatic pilot. As much as possible, stay alert and in the anticipatory mode all waking hours, no matter at home, or in public. The kids have a phrase that really fits here-"Stay in the moment and check-it-all-out".

- **Don't' be embarrassed to ask for help.** Mostly people love to feel helpful. It may become the high point in a day that's routine. Even good cocktail or dinner talk. Can you hear it? "I helped this elderly woman up into the bus, or I made sure this elderly gent crossed the road safely. (He/She) didn't have to try it on their own." The Good Samaritan earns what we used to call brownie points and the regard of their peers. So don't be embarrassed...ask or just accept help!

- **Safe not Sorry.** If there are two ways to get somewhere or do something and always assuming you see the difference - choose the way you know is safe, rather than the one that is quicker, or nearer. It's likely to be much more risky.

- **The matter of RUSHING.** It's one of the most consistent and hazardous mistakes for older citizens! It causes trips and falls, obviates care and self-protection, encourages mindless activity, and almost always leads to trouble.

Now, how to encapsulate and make useful all of the above? Believe it or not it's a simple "3 Look Method".

The 3 Look Method

Think of the times you've gotten in trouble or even hurt. Isn't it possible you've said to yourself, "If I'd only looked to see, or listened for, or taken my time?" Need I say more?

But how do you teach yourself to do this consistently?

The way you teach yourself any new thing you must master or remember- by constant and deliberate repetition. If you're one who never goes to sleep without an evening prayer, it's a simple extension of that habit, making these simple words in effect your 'morning invocation' - **STOP, LOOK, AND LISTEN!**

First, **Stop** (or pause) for a moment before entering, new, or unfamiliar surroundings.

Second **Listen**, always give a quick listen for any strange or warning sounds.

Third **Look,** I don't mean a glance or peek. I mean really look! There is a deliberate method to looking, you may not have thought about, but it will protect you in any circumstance.

3 Look Method in Action:

STEP 1: LOOK LOW
At floor, street or rug level.

STEP 2: LOOK LEVEL
At chair–level or mid-point of objects possibly in your way.

STEP 3: LOOK UP
Towards ceilings, lighting or sky.

Practice it over and over, and do it consistently - whether in old familiar or brand new circumstances. If you use it

routinely, you are at least 90% at your safe-not-sorry-goal.
(Except accidents beyond our control, so no 100%)
Now having dealt with general principles, we can go on
to the specifics of Slip and Fall prevention.

In each section I'll try to use **The 3 Look Method** as I hope
you will. It makes for both consistency, and system- two
entirely desirable safety techniques.

It may seem a lot to think about. But actually as a
invocation, it can be a new skill you learn helping you
each and every night and day. As you use it more, and
more it will get both easier, and more effective.

If you read this chapter carefully, you may note that I've
offered you capital "A" solid advice, but we all know in
actuality advice is one of the hardest things to give or
receive...I've never been sure why this is so, but I do know
that it is possibly because no one likes a wisenheimer.

The only thing that might modify this reaction for you is to
tell you I do actually follow my own program. So to iterate
Stop, Look, and Listen, you may truly avoid an event both
you and your dear ones wish had never happened. A Slip
and Fall.

JOURNAL

_____

_____

_____

_____

_____

_____

_____

_____

_____

_____

_____

_____

_____

CHAPTER 3
PERSONAL EFFECTS

- Staying in the Moment
- Everyday Basics

Staying in the Moment

We know safety starts in general with staying in the moment, and therefore being aware of your surroundings and the hazards they may present at all times.

What is meant by staying in the moment has been expressed in many ways, many of which will be familiar to you. Don't try to throw before you've caught the ball, keep focus in what's right in front of you - daydreaming is great, but wait till you've reached a safe perch before indulging. One thing at a time. I could go on, but I think you get the concept. It's critical to your safety and wellbeing.

Distraction is invariably a serious enemy of safe and sound. It is to be avoided at any and every moment. Also consider the lesson of the hare and the tortoise, slow but sure wins the day.

Personal independence depends primarily on controlling our personal space or surroundings. The 3 Look Method is a very good part of staying in the moment, and controlling our space.

Also, there are excellent mechanical aids which if needed, help keep you from being distracted, such as a cane, a walker, an extended grabber, or a cell phone. Especially consider the extraordinary value of a medic alert device ideally worn on your person.

Here are some other specific thoughts:

The Matter of What you Wear.
Believe it or not what you wear can be a safety issue. Note it is possible to be chic and still not sorry.

Shoes
- ✓ Consider reserving high heels for parties. Optimally- wear no more than 2 inches for every day.
- ✓ Wear what you can put on easily.
- ✓ Non-slip soles.
- ✓ Extra Long shoe horn and a device (sock aid) to help put on your stockings.

Clothing
- ✓ Things easy to put on and get off. Openings in the front, unless you have a nimble fingered partner. And zippers rather than those small, tough buttons.
- ✓ Wear warm enough clothing and coats in the winter seasons. Cold can distract.
- ✓ Protect your fingers and ears in season.

✓ Waterproof shoe coverings with no slip soles for bad weather.

Outerwear - not too heavy or difficult to put on.
✓ All Weatherproof
✓ 30% of body heat is lost through the head- so think about hats or caps or hoodies.
✓ When push comes to shove, better that you're warm and protected against the elements than a fashion plate.

Every Day Basics

We all seem to be in a rush as soon as we start our days. As an everyday matter don't rush when getting up or crossing a room. Stand for a moment on rising to insure your balance. Once up, consider whether you would be better off using a cane or other lateral support then venturing across the room unsteadily.

Develop a routine for what, when, and how you do things. For example: Let's us suppose you are going to your mailbox for your mail - Make it a routine to remember the basics-

- Dress appropriately for its location.
- Make sure you have your door and mailbox keys with you.
- If late afternoon or evening, turn all lights on.
- Get up easily, and balance for a moment.
- If you expect packages, choose a chair or table near the door to put them down on for the moment, and ask for help if you think you'll need it for heavy or awkward pieces.

If you wake up and find its cold and wet outside, and you feel more achy than usual, take it as an extra warning sign that you're that much more Slip and Fall prone. This may be a good day to use what has been called **a get up and go test** or at least my version.

The point of this exercise is it shows you clearly and physically what your common sense tells you should be so. It's a quick gait and balance assessment. So before you start off – check yourself. If you have any question in your mind that one of these is 'off' – sit down again, take a few deep breaths and re-try. In all likelihood if you do this, the second go through will yield better results, with safety and balance.

The Get up and Go Test:
1. Can you get up from a chair using your hands or arms only lightly?
2. Can you get up, walk 6 paces turn and return to your chair without staggering or feeling woozy.
3. Can you stand; close your eyes for a moment without losing balance.
4. Do you feel steady on your feet, and do you remain so after taking several steps.

Remember always rise from a sitting or lying position slowly, letting the world equilibrate - especially after doing things like tying your shoes, or reaching for an object on the floor.

Your General Physical Condition.
No matter how, habitual or minimal this thought, give it some respect, and at least some attention. It really makes a difference.

- Don't overtire yourself or over do.
- Eat healthily
- Try to do some exercises at a regular time every day. (See the exercise choices in chapter 9).

We know that chances are we are not going to achieve the condition of our twenties, or by and large become marathoners, but on the other hand, you are not excused to become a couch or chair potato.

Partnered Activities

When possible outside your home, (for movies, theater, church, and sports events or the like), partner up.

Consider - the buddy system is a must for scuba diving, even used by great and athletic swimmers. As a matter of fact, it is <u>required</u> by every legitimate sea diving group. Trouble can arrive unexpectedly, and having a buddy to help out may make the difference between survival and non-survival - if these superb athletes partner up, why not us.

Medical Issues do Bear Directly on Slip and Falls.

If you haven't paid attention to your present medical condition you are asking for serious trouble. This is really a no brainer as your kids, or partner or even your MD will tell you. So....

- Schedule regular MD visits.
- Don't forget your dentist.
- Yearly oculist check-up.
- Bi-yearly auditory testing.

During your MD visit, review your current medications. If you've had recent surgery, have the follow up visits as indicated by the surgeon's office. I know all this seems a lot of MDing, but it pays off every time as your physician will tell you and it will relieve the minds of your near and dear.

Post-Surgery – Special Circumstances

While we're on the subject of the personal, there are some special circumstances. Research has indicated that post- surgery people are more vulnerable to a Slip-and-

Fall than they may have been pre-op.

The reasons for this are many-general weakness, pain, meds, lack of sleep, newness of some functions that were previously automatic. In other words, as a post op patient on return home - you must be doubly careful. Use all the above strategies to avoid trouble.

Information Please
It is smart, and also kindly to let one of your near and dear know what you are planning each day in terms of activities both in and out of the house.

- They may wish to help or you may wish them to help with some.
- If a problem arises they know where to find you.
- Try to let them know the day before so planning becomes efficient.

These are some of the personal effects that have occurred to me. I would like to suggest that you think about your own thoughts and additions, and note them in your journal pages adding to this chapter.

 **JOURNAL**

_____

_____

_____

_____

_____

_____

_____

_____

_____

_____

_____

_____

_____

_____

_____

CHAPTER 4
HAZARDS AT HOME

- Create and Maintain a Safe Environment
- Room-by-Room Safety

Create and Maintain a Safe Environment

Whether you own a rose covered cottage, a condo, a walk up rental, or even a Mcmansion, It's HOME.

Home has always been considered a virtual nest of safety. However, this is not always the case. Anticipating what may prove to be dangerous, I have tried to be as inclusive as possible in these suggestions. Some of them may not apply to your personal nest. But, look at all of them and simply cross-out those that are not germane.

To create and maintain a safe nest is best accomplished by logical and deliberate steps consistently using the 3 Look Method of Chapter two.

Just as a reminder of the 3 Look Method – look down towards your footing, look level for objects in the way, look up for adequate lighting, before you become an active part of a scene.

Make it a practice to do this each and every time you come into an area, particularly if you've just changed something around in a room - you never want to be on automatic pilot.

- ✓ Check footing in an area that typically undergoes changes e.g. an area that's been rained on, been waxed, or sported new rugs etc. etc. etc.
- ✓ AND remember – you - may have changed e.g. today using a cane, new glasses, or having an unusually bad arthritic day (due to cold and wet weather.)

Special notes:

What happens to these areas in rain or snow? Take special precautions in the event of inclement weather.

- ▪ Plan your foot wear and clothing
- ▪ Ask about snow clearance
- ▪ Note: your umbrella can always double as a cane.
- ▪ Take a cane that you might not need in good weather.

Room-by-Room Safety

Getting From the Outside – In

Step l: (Look Low) Observe steps, sidewalks or pathways.

- Look for uneven places,
  - ✓ cracks,
  - ✓ raised areas,
  - ✓ areas under repair
- Look for what type of surface you're dealing with (Cement? Marble, uneven ground? Etc.)
- Look for what type entrance.
  - ✓ Does the entrance have a turnstile door,
  - ✓ Is it heavy or tough to move, requiring two hands – is it too difficult for one person.
  - ✓ Does the door offer an 'automatic' opener?
  - ✓ Is the entrance keyed (and how to un-key it).

Step 2: (Look Level) Look for any areas under construction or renovation.

- Are there steps or stairways to negotiate?
  - ✓ What kind of surfaces?
  - ✓ Are there railings that can help?
  - ✓ What is under repair?

Step 3: (Look Up) Look at any areas above or up.

- Be sure lighting is adequate to negotiate your entrance.
  - ✓ Is the area bright enough?
  - ✓ Do you have to turn anything on?

✓ Make sure overhead area is clear, so as to not hit your head.

Garage – (a special area)

✓ Entrance and exits (Be sure your remote is easily available.)
✓ Do you have to turn on lighting?
✓ Check flooring, of course.
✓ If you have a key that lights the car and opens the door remotely, get it ready as soon as you enter the garage or parking lot.

Inside the Home

Vestibules or Hallways

Step 1 (Look Low)

- Condition of the carpeting or rugs.
- Any steps to be negotiated.
- Any washing or waxing going on.

Step 2 (Look level)

- Has any furniture been moved or changed?
- Is the elevator working and its lighting good?
- Don't forget railings are there for your use.

Step 3: (Look Up)

- Is the lighting in these areas good?
- Do you need to turn switches on or off, and where are these located?

- Replace home lighting or inform management of any lighting outages.

The Elevator (a special area)

- Do you know emergency procedures should the elevator get stuck?
- Are the floor stops clearly marked?
- Report any malfunction however minor (Elevator stop not be completely level with exit surface etc.)
- Which stairways to use in case of outage, their lighting and handrails.

Every day, every room Hazards.

Now as you go from room-to-room there are invariable hazards that are identical, so instead of detailing each challenge, we will simply remind you with a single word. Each time you see it, it will subsume the following:

Lighting:

- Do you know how the lighting is controlled? Can you switch it on BEFORE you enter the room?
- Did you leave some form of light on before you left?
- Is the wattage sufficient for the area?
- Are there any outages and were they replaced?
- Do you know the replacement or notification procedures for outages?
- Have you had any "shorts" in the past and have these shorts been corrected?

- If you have a pet do you know where it is when you enter the room?

Flooring:

- Rugs (with or without nonskid backing) and small area rugs (a real Slip and Fall hazard should be eliminated). As should high pile carpeting or rugs.
- Be aware of flooring materials-wood, marble are they slippery or uneven?
- Clear pathways to commonly used places (e.g. living room to Bedroom, bathroom or door).
- Any recent waxing or repair?
  PS. If repair is needed in your own home, take control- and schedule these as not to become a Slip and Fall hazard.

Wiring:

- Beware of any tortuous or ill covered wiring like under carpets etc.
- Any wiring to an appliance you can trip on.
- Any shorts?
- Try to bunch wires where possible. Add a surge protector to help you organize wires and wiring.
- No 'nest' of wires...organize.

Special Features for Where You Spend your Time

If you are like most people who spend a lot of time at home, you have your favorite chair, room, or daily routine. Within these areas I am offering tips to take advantage of them. One example is the table that invariably resides next to your favorite chair or sitting place.

Now all this has been very detailed, and may seem overwhelming. You can't learn all of this at one time, and have any expectation of retaining it so…..

- Concentrate on the important aspects of your most important functional centers first
- Take one area at a time to study and learn
- Don't be upset if you have to learn it more than once.
- Sit somewhere both centered and secure as your studying post.

Living Room

- Easy wall switch for all lamps in room.
- The ideal lamp is one that responds to hand-clap.
- Furniture room layout- create easy paths from one spot to another.
- Wiring should be tucked under carpet or at least out of walking paths.

Remember:

- ✓ Check the Lighting
- ✓ Check the Flooring
- ✓ Check the Wiring

BATHROOM
Equipment considerations: The bathroom is an area that will reward special attention - it can be VERY hazardous.

- Get a raised toilet seat (easy to rise and sit).

- Install and use grab bars in shower, bathtub, and by side of toilet seat.
- Keep soap on a rope for showering in a convenient place.
- Put non-slip rubber matting in shower and/or bath tub.
- Place critical toiletries and dental care products on countertops, not under counters.
- If medications are to be kept in bathroom, keep all in one organized container and refill weekly.

Remember:

✓ Check the Lighting
✓ Check the Flooring
✓ Check the Wiring

BEDROOM

- Install night lights (they must be replaced about every 8 months).
- Critical - Is there a clear pathway from bed to bathroom?
- Pick a consistent and easy area to change into and out of bedclothes.
- Keep extra blankets within easy reach of bed.
- Use loose sheets for easy egress from bed.
- Pre-think book, television schedule, and remote, location before you get into bed.

Remember:

✓ Check the Lighting

✓ Check the Flooring
✓ Check the Wiring

DINING ROOM

- Check there is enough area, around the table to be easily negotiable.
- Be sure you can handle the chairs.
- Low nap or no rugs.

Remember:

✓ Check the Lighting
✓ Check the Flooring
✓ Check the Wiring

KITCHEN

- Keep a grabber for high or hard to get objects.
- Keep favorite pots and pans at an easy level, or easy to reach area.
- Raise pet bowls (water and food) off floor.
- Clean liquid spills up immediately. No "I'll take care of it later".
- Stock up on frozen foods against possible home bound conditions (either health or weather).

Remember:

✓ Check the Lighting
✓ Check the Flooring
✓ Check the Wiring

If you've done most of this, you've gone a long way to securing your own safety. And home has regained much of its nest- like character. As you spot any unique features, add them to the list at the end of this chapter immediately, don't wait to see if you remember them once you've finished reading this.

Special Areas or Items

Chair-side or bedside vicinities:

- Lamps- are they easily reached and do they have adequate wattage?
- Are your cell phone and land lines kept within easy reach?
- A medic-alert necklace (Should be purchased and used).
- TV remote (If it's across the room, it may be no help when you want it).
- A list of critical drugs and medical conditions charted –and available within reach.
- Who to notify in emergencies – again - available within reach.
- Keep your daily medications preferably in a box or container organized by days of the week, if not completed in bathroom.

The Matter of a Cell phone
The money spent on a cell phone is worth its weight in gold. Here are a few thoughts:

- Try to carry it on your person in an easily reachable and consistent place, or alternatively in your purse.

- Load it with telephone numbers of:
  - ✓ Your primary caregiver.
  - ✓ Your nearest and most reliable family members or friends.
  - ✓ Your primary physician.
  - ✓ Emergency or 911.
  - ✓ Just in case...don't forget your own.

Most important – be sure you have been shown 'how' to use your cell phone and its features. Remember it has to be plugged in overnight.

Locomotion

Moving about from place-to-place.

Normally we devote absolutely no thought to how we move in the familiar environment of our own home. After all, we set it up, are more than familiar with its features, and have been comfortable and secure even moving from here-to-there in the darkness for many years. TRUE. However as we age this can no longer be taken for granted with impunity.

So... some considerations to help restore safety while moving about within your domicile.

- Don't rush. Get up slowly and let your balance equilibrate, especially if there has been any recent change in your regular medication.
- Before you move take a quick look around for loose objects or new hazards.
- Wear flat, rubber soled shoe ware.

- Don't move about in the dark or even semi-dark – light it up!

Transporting things from place-to-place

- Don't try to carry everything in one trip.
- Divide packages and/or objects into separate, manageable lots.
- Make sure your path is clear and turn on lights even before venturing.

Remember stairs are one of the major hazards both at home and abroad. All too many accidents happen involving stairs.

- Make sure you see or light up the entire staircase before you mount or descend it.
- Check its surfaces and your shoe wear carefully.
- Use the hand rails.
- Consider installing reflective tape on the hard-leading edges where possible.

JOURNAL

_____

_____

_____

_____

_____

_____

_____

_____

_____

_____

_____

_____

_____

- Planes, Trains, Automobiles and More

Planes, Trains, Automobiles and More

Hazards abroad mean anything from your front yard, to your church, from a street crossing, to an airport. Abroad from your home base is hazardous just because it can be unfamiliar.

As you travel from your home remember the three steps of inspection (LOW, LEVEL And UP) as they are more important than ever. And I would add, **always Listen** for the unexpected (from an approaching vehicle, to alerting signals (sirens, bells, whistles etc.).

I've outlined things below for your consideration, but there are always others that can happen. So, add to your entries, as you experience them.

- SIGHT: Your sight and therefore your eye glasses become very important. Be sure you are secure with both at distance and close up.
    - ✓ Are your glasses cleaned?

- ✓ I like to see glasses worn on a necklace arrangement-hard to forget, close at hand, and harder to drop.
- ✓ Is your eye prescription up to date, when was your last check-up?

- CLOTHING: Watch what you wearing. Safety before chic - going abroad starts when you decide what to wear to go out. Coats, gloves and hats when appropriate are no brainers, but consider long and hard your shoes, flowy, and overlong attire.

- WEATHER: In inclement weather shoes should be non- skid and flat. However in normal weather the flat and rubber soles suggestion is still good. If you are attending a social affair, you can always CARRY a pair of party shoes to be put on when you arrive.

Okay, out into the Crowds.

Crowd Control

Crowds can present problems – hustling, bumping, texting, or overactive arguments, and participants.

- Look, listen and evaluate before entering into a crowd.
- Consider using a cane or wheelchair, even if normally you don't (you may have to stand or walk for greater periods than normal). It also lets other know you need space.

- Try to schedule trips, even shopping, or movies during <u>off</u> hours.
- Remember the advantages of the buddy system - try to avoid solo trips.
- Always inform someone responsible where, when and how long you will be.

Get used to taking your phone, medical alert, and medical emergency information card with you.

Do not be surprised if activities in a crowded or public venue are fatiguing. It takes more out of anyone to negotiate the crowded or unfamiliar.

Take your time if walking longer distances. Very often a wayside bench or chair can be found to let you rest for a moment – it will add immeasurably to your endurance.

Buses and Trains
Think out the trip and conveyances before you leave home. It is more than worthwhile to eliminate en route surprises. Check out, money, printed schedule routes, and tickets.

- The first or entering step to a train or bus can be a large one - use the hand rails, and ask for help if needed. Often if you're with cane etc., the bus can 'kneel'.
- Carry only things (bags, backpacks etc.) that you can handle, hands free.
- Get help for larger baggage either professional (porters) or your traveling companion or even a willing stranger.

- Keep tickets and boarding cards in an easily available pocket or section of carry-all or backpack.
- Subways may present a problem, especially if they're crowded. Look for poles, overhead straps and handles, and above all a kindly soul likely to give up a seat.
- On long train trips, sit relatively near to the lavatory, and plan to use it only during stops. Often they are found near the car exit/entrance.

Airlines and Airports

I strongly advise use of a wheelchair for airports. The distances from curb to check-in, and again from security to boarding areas are often extended. Any airline will arrange a curb-side wheel chair if you inform them when booking your ticket, (for both departure and arrival.)

If you use a wheelchair, the attendant who wheels you can be very helpful going through security. (often taking you right to the head of the line!)

Unlike the advice about crowds during shopping, theater, movies and so on, with airlines and any long distance traveling, book travel during frequent hours, (so help is most likely to be available).

- Book aisle seats as far forward (toward exits) as possible.
- Let the airline stewards help you with overhead luggage, on first seating and debarking.
- If you can elevate feet during flight do so.

- Drink lots of water, but eat lightly.
- Arrange to be met by friends, or relatives, if possible.
- Phone or email your near and dear and let them know you have arrived intact.

When you use Cars

- Get into a vehicle whenever possible, rear-end first.
- If you're driving, set the seat maximally back before entering, and after entering adjust to driving position.
- Then check and if necessary reset your mirrors, side and rear before turning the ignition on.
- Make sure car is in park, when you start up and stop.
- Be sure you know the windshield wipers, lights, and dashboard controls.
- Keep up-to-date insurance cards, car registration in the glove box compartment and know exactly how to get emergency help should you need it.

As to how you get there

- Think out your route of travel before you engage motor.
- Leave plenty of time to get to your destination.
- Travel with a buddy whenever you can, and if needed let him be co-pilot, and co-observer.

Walking Streets
Consider streets as serious potential problem areas. Be prepared to do constant stop, look, and listening.

- Pavements can be uneven or even broken.
- Look ahead for any problems or hazards along your walking route.
- Be especially alert negotiating curbs.
- Avoid hurry.
- Do not carry large or heavy objects if possible.
- Leave time to cross a street without having to rush or get caught in the middle.
- Locate overhead signals.

Theaters and Churches

- In church (temple), look for aisle seats.
- Watch for tricky footing, especially with the pew kneelers.
- If you're taking communion, wait till most parishioners have gone forward.

As to theater...here are a few tips:

- Try to seat yourself last if you have an aisle seat, but first if you have a middle of the row seat.
- Exit the theater last, letting the crowds get out of your way and allow the lights to come on.
- Use toilet facilities before you attend, rather than during the movie.
- Enter before lights go down. This means at the movies, you'll have to sit thru all those previews.

Attention Homeowners

- Make sure that repairs or maintenance of the pathways to front and rear doors are up to snuff.

- Is the lighting all working?
- Have you scheduled snow clearance?
- Are the hand rails in good repair?
- Self-locking door knobs may present extra problems. Hide a key as a just in case.
- I tend to wear my front door key around my neck when I go out, but this is not everyone's sense of style.

JOURNAL

CHAPTER 6
NO FOOLING PRACTICAL MEASURES

6

- Practical Solutions
- Strategies to Increase Your Safety Odd

Practical Solutions

Some of these practical solutions we've noted in conjunction with specific locations, but I'd also like to give you some of the 'no fooling BASIC practical measures to follow.'

Planning and Actions

Some of these may strike you as fuddy-duddy or offend your vanity - if so pick and choose, but as a practicing Physician for more than 30 years, I at least, HAVE COME TO observe and appreciate many of these.

Consider having on hand at all times:
- A fanny-pack or stomach - pack containing
- **ID cards (Social security, and drivers for example)**
- **Another plastic covered card with**
  - ✓ Your name, address and phone number
  - ✓ The person to notify in case of emergency
  - ✓ Your most serious medical conditions and medications.

- ✓ Your most serious allergies (especially to penicillin products.)
- ✓ Your Medicare or other insurance name and number.
- ✓ Your MD phone number.

All of this list should be done in duplicate (one to keep for your pack and one to lose), and plasticized, so as not to be torn, melted or otherwise vitiated. (Any Staples or Office Max etc. will do this for you.)

I think the reason for this is pretty obvious, but consider the case if you are not able to answer for yourself, either due to injury, illness or temporary loss of memory.

Cell phone
Make sure preloaded with the numbers of:

- your emergency person
- your home number
- your physician's number

They are your guaranteed link to help, and communication. I can't overemphasize their usefulness.

- Keep your cell phone charged.
- When the phone indicates low, recharge immediately.
- Store and know how to use stored essential numbers so that should you need them, help is easily reached.

Purchase a Cane

I bet you'll say but I don't need one! And perhaps you don't under most circumstances. But consider if you have had, or are a candidate for any, hip or knee surgery, or have begun to have weakness or pain anywhere due to arthritis, or if you have any diminution of sight or coordination - a cane may be the smartest thing you can do to protect yourself in the Slip and Fall prevention department.

Consider this too- a cane may serve to warn others not to expect you to be speedy Gonzalez, and to give you a little wiggle room in a crowded situation.

I might add as a matter of style, for many years a cane was considered a sign of elegance with both Male and Female attire. For you scotch drinkers think of the image on the bottle of the upscale Johnny Walker Black Scotch brand.

Finally, in the ideational 'belt and suspenders' department even if this is not something you want to think about, consider if you have any degree of arthritis, aren't there some mornings, when you honestly think a cane would really be a help.

The question arises then-Do you know how to select a cane? Here are some suitability features.

How to Select a Cane

- (Height)- the crook or curve of the cane should lie at wrist level when the arm is at your side.

- The foot or base should be rubberized, a non-slip type.
- It should be sturdy, not just for decoration.
- I would suggest that you have more than one:
  - ✓ In the umbrella stand by the front door (or its equivalent).
  - ✓ By your favorite chair.
  - ✓ By your bedside.

I personally keep a folding cane in my car in anticipation of all I might not have anticipated.

However, if you get caught outdoors and happen to have one, your umbrella makes a good emergency cane. And alerts as we noted before people to give you space.

As to cost, I believe your medical insurance covers canes.

Crutches

Let's face it, no one likes crutches. But…vanity has no place here. If you need them, you need them- for balance and stability.

They should be carefully chosen and measured. I prefer Canadian or Lofstrand for my patients. (These fit over your forearm, rather than seated in your armpit).

The traditional under the armpit models, can cause nerve damage because of weight placed on the arm pieces, and if not this, they tend to cause irritation to the axillae (arm pit) and I can't tell you how often I've seen people with all kinds of cloths and materials wrapped around the arm pieces, in the attempt to soften the discomfort of undue weight on the axillae, (which anatomically has all kinds of major nerves and vessels coursing through them).

Let a pro fit you! (MD, PT, or crutch issuer)

A Walker

You may find these more stable and secure than cane or crutches. If you feel you need one in order to get around safely, the chances are you are right.

- Check that the height is right for you. (With surgical supply store, physical therapist or visiting nurse). The walker should be above wrist height when you stand.
- Get a sturdy walker rather, than inexpensive walker.
- Many are folding - easy to store when not in use.

And Medicare generally covers their cost.

An Object Grabber

That's one of those devices you see in the supermarket used by the employees to get an object down from a high shelf. There's a pincher at the end of the stick. Good for tough shelves and high closets at home also things that may have fallen and you can't get to.

A Pocket or Keychain Flashlight

There are so many uses for this small tool it's hard to know where to start. Here are a few suggestions. Get the one with extended batteries, and a significantly bright light (your local hardware store stocks and can give good advice.) It is easy to carry around, and is one of the most important 'on my person' tools in preventing trouble. If the light switch is off or not locatable, and it's dark, you needn't be in darkness for long.

- Keep flashlight in purse or pocket.
- One by bedside and one on the table next to your favorite chair.
- One in an easy place to spot and remember in the kitchen as well.
- A keychain flashlight that lights the lock at night is also a good idea for dark entrances.

Strategies to Increase Your Safety Odds

Deliberate and Consistent Notification
Someone close to you should be informed of your plans for the day. Could be child, spouse, lover, relative, friend, boss etc. etc. It's important that when, and where you plan to be is known by someone who can do something about it if you don't show up where, and when you're supposed to be.

The Deal with Medications and Prescriptions
As we age we tend to accumulate medications. Many may be out of date or unnecessary. Generally speaking these may be prescription based drugs.

Take Action.
- Keep a memo to contact your physician on a regular basis to ensure they remain appropriate.

- Keep a list of what they are, and when they must be renewed, and be sure someone in the family also has this list.
- Pay attention to renewal dates! Arrange for pick-up or delivery as indicated by renewal date.
- You may want to establish YOUR pharmacy - one that you will use regularly, (so that the pharmacist is familiar with your prescriptions, any side effects, and renewal dates is the real benefit of such an arrangement).
- Keep all medications in a place where you will not fail to see and take them. If you have specific meds for emergency-only (e.g. nitro glycerin, adrenaline), that are best kept:
  - ✓ on your person,
  - ✓ or the table where you generally sit,
  - ✓ or in an easily seen spot in your bathroom.

The Before I Leave my House List (a Mental aid)

The 'before I leave my house list' is an unbelievably helpful safety tool. Make a list of essentials to be carried on your person when you leave your house. Get them copied in triplicate, and plasticized. Keep the list on the table or chest nearest the front door AND check it before you leave.

Sample List

- Name, address, telephone home, medical allergies, and emergency contact printed on a card.

- Daily medications – essential Meds you need to take during the day or in case of known emergencies.
- Medical insurance cards.
- Cell phone.
- Medical alert.
- Tickets or passes as needed.
- Credit card/minimal amount of cash.
- Pocket flashlight.
- Key ring (both auto and house keys).

The Issue of Pets

- Walking and feeding routines should be known not only to you but someone who sees you regularly. If needed post the routines on wall next to where your pet regularly eats.
- Regular grooming and veterinarian needs also can be listed.
- Identify a surrogate pet-care-person in case you are at all disabled. (Even colds and arthritic flare-ups count).
- The posted pet list:
  - ✓ Food details (what, how often and treats).
  - ✓ Walking habits.
  - ✓ Vet's name, telephone number and address.
  - ✓ Grooming routine.

You may find a large dog too much for you to handle. Such a development can provide trouble. So think about the pet you pick as you get older.

The last thing we all wish is for a pet that is uncared for; if for one reason or another we are not able to do so. So think of your pet before yourself, if you become ill or disabled - the home he needs may not be yours.

The Get Up and Go Test

There may be days when you wake up to extra joint pain or dizziness, even just a feeling of general malaise or weakness. It's hard to quantify or measure these feelings, but they're legitimate and deserve some respect. Anyone who says they don't have some of these off days is countering common sense, sensibility, and reality.

So - on these days don't hesitate to modify the quantity and quality of your own body demands. It's not self-pampering, nothing to be ashamed of or be embarrassed by. All medical pros know it can happen. But a word to the wise, if it persists beyond a day or so, you mustn't ignore it as it may be the start of a permanent health change. So should a 'bad-day' become a 'few bad days', inform your MD.

One way to help objectify and assess this kind of happening is fairly simple. Essentially it consists of an evaluation of the state of your balance and muscular strength. There are many versions of this assessment, here's mine.

The Get Up and Go Test (From chair-to-stand, and go-ability)

1. Sit in a chair. Then - can you stand up without using your hands or with little assistance from them?
2. Once up-Can you stand steady with your arms folded or at your side?
3. Stand up - close your eyes for a moment- are you steady on your pins? Or do you have to widen your stance or eyes to maintain your balance?
4. Walk away a short distance, then turn. Can you come back to your chair with no difficulty?
5. Is your gait even and without hesitation or stagger?

Now, grade yourself. An A would be all steps okay. An F would be if you couldn't do either step 1 or 2. You want to be at least a B or B+ (able to do steps 1-4).

Try this before you go ahead with your normal day, and especially if you plan any kind of excursion that involves leaving the house.

The Most Important Learning Trick of All - Balance

"I lost my balance" is another phrase we hear over and over when talking about Slip and Falls. And indeed balance becomes less than automatic as we age. Knowing this - it may well be the precursor to a fall - the question is what can be done about it?

The Three Point Stance

Try this for balance. (Also don't confuse this stance with the pose football linemen assume before the football snap.)

Teach yourself to use it consistently when you have to stand up for any length of time. As you rise be sure one foot faces straight ahead while the other is placed to its side at 90 degrees (creating an "L").

Your feet should be shoulder width apart. Those of you who are familiar with ballet will recognize this stance as 'third position'. Once you stand take a breath and let everything equilibrate.

ILLUSTRATION OF THREE POINT STANCE

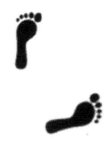

The three point stance is often the answer to achieving and maintaining consistent and reliable balance. If you teach yourself to use it consistently every time you rise from a sitting or lying position it will really make the difference, and let you feel, and be steady.

Well there are exercises that work on balance, and these help. But is there something that can be used every day, in every condition? Fortunately there is – the Three Point Stance!

I CANNOT EMPHASIZE TOO STRONGLY HOW EFFECTIVE THE THREE POINT STANCE IS IN ESTABLISHING IMMEDIATE BALANCE AND MAINTAINING IT, BEFORE YOU GO INTO MOTION.

A Few Leftovers
Now that we've explored many of the specific ways to prevent "accidents from happening in specific venues, and during specific times, and now you've been exposed, or even re-exposed to some of life's challenges

to you , here are some organizational and general leftover thoughts.

Neatness counts

I happen to be a casual liver in my own home. Things have rarely been organized or regularized. However in the world of Slip and Fall, neatness does count. Therefore make the extra, if not entertaining effort to store things away, pick things up and organize to the best of your ability so they have not the slightest opportunity to become unexpected 'hazards'.

- **A Few Left Over Specifics**
  Replace high pile with low pile carpeting. **(High pile is a real trip and fall menace).**
- Consider installing double handrails on free standing stairways.
- Where and when possible get rid of area rugs.
- Be sure your freezer is always well stocked with the three food groups (meat, vegetable, fruit) as there may be times when if for no other reason you are house-bound, due to such things as inclement weather.
- Check that the mechanical things in your household are in good repair. The last thing you need is for the furnace to go out in winter months or the AC in hot summer.
- If you're a home owner especially in the country consider the purchase of a generator.

JOURNAL

_____

_____

_____

_____

_____

_____

_____

_____

_____

_____

_____

_____

_____

_____

_____

CHAPTER 7
ABOUT MEDICATIONS AND MDs

About Medications and MDs

We all have been told over and over to check the side effects of the medications we take. Our pharmacist tells us and distributes an elaborate pamphlet each time he fills a prescription. (Unfortunately, it's written in fly speck font, but it does tell us all that is known about the chemical make-up, and side effects).

If you are like many of my patients, not only is it hard to read, but it's written in medicalease, a language which you may not be conversant.

Our doctors also tell us there are always side effects to a medication, and even TV infomercials and ads announce major side effects.

If however you're like many people, as we age we seem to aggregate vials and bottle of pills that we take on a regular basis, but forget to check back with our MDs about them. We need to review medications either once a year, or if we begin to develop a reaction to one - report it. Your MD will willingly go over your Meds, if for no other reason to avoid having to deal with a serious adverse reaction you may present him.

Here is one more serious concern. Various medications may have different side-effects <u>when taken together</u>. I think without question that any change in medication, or change in your reaction to them should be thoroughly checked out by your MD.

You can certainly help as the person most concerned and most familiar with your own reactions to them.

Check off list

- Do I still need each and every medication?
- Has my reaction to any of them changed?
- Do I 'feel' perhaps the dosage is too high or too low?
- Have I developed any kind of allergic reaction?
- Are they all up to date (not expired)?

Side effects

Okay. But what of these side effects - what in general are they? It would be impossible to parse out the whole pharmacopeia or drugs we take, but here is a list of some common medications, and common side effects.

Common Medication Side Effects	Medication Type
Dizziness	Anti-convulsants, anti-depressants narcotics (Pain killers), neuroleptics (Tranquillizers)
Drowsiness	Anti-convulsants, anti-depressants narcotics (Pain killers), neuroleptics (Tranquillizers)
Confusion	Anti-convulsants, anti-depressants narcotics (Pain killers), neuroleptics (Tranquillizers) - plus anti-cholinergic (Bronchodilators)
Gait disturbances	Anti-depressants, neuroleptics Metoclopramides (anti-heartburn and reflux)
Problems with Balance	Neuroleptic, anticonvulsants, benzodiazepines (anti-anxiety Meds)
Visual disturbances	Neuroleptics and Anticholinergics
Faintness(syncope)	Vasodilators,(beta blockers- anti high blood pressure, nitrates, vasodilators
GI Disturbance or Burning	Many Meds which help with pain are harsh on stomach. May even cause bleeding.

I'm pretty sure that on first read of this chapter you may sigh and think to yourself, is all this necessary?

Seems a lot to remember, seems a lot to do, and plan for. And you're right. So it is. But with faithful repetition, it will seem easier and easier. Remember when you first learned to drive a car- how many things both intrinsic and extrinsic you had to think about and train yourself to remember and do? But with time and repetition, most of it has become automatic, and second nature.

Once you get used using the check off list, it goes quickly, and you have helped yourself to a real safety net.

This is a very brief list. The simplest thing to do is take pen and paper on your next visit to your MD. Ask him about the most common side effects for the drugs you are given, and if he has recorded any adverse reactions you may have had in the past to any one of them. And write them down (the act of writing tends to embed them in memory).

The Vital Role of your MD

As a physician, I can tell you no doctor wants to hear second hand his patient has fallen or slipped and sustained a serious injury. Not because it may create problems for him, but because we care, and don't want to receive such bad news, especially if it could have been avoided!

Therefore, use your MD to help prevent these injuries with:

- **A regular visit to your GP or internist.**
  I can't emphasize how important this is. It lets your MD adjust medications, suggest activities, assess medically your current state, and update any further suggestions about your health and well-being.

- **Regular visits to your podiatrist.**
  If your feet hurt or are developing problems, it affects not only your gait and security while walking, but even your balance. He will treat what may be causing problems, and is an expert on the kind of shoe wear you should be using. It is he, who will write an RX for specially made shoes (especially important for diabetics with foot problems).

  A great philosopher once said "Give *me a place* on which to *stand*, and I *will* move the Earth." You may not wish to move the world, but the importance of your feet and stance is clear.

- **Regular Visits to your Dentist**
  Health threatening infections after surgery involving any prosthesis, or hardwire insertion can happen. What occurs is that the bacteria which reside in your mouth may infect these many months or even years after the surgery. So you want to take the antibiotic of your dentist's suggestion prior to your visit. Prevention of 'seeding' from your mouth to the surgical site is critical.

If you have serious dental problems (with dentures, loose teeth, gum disease) - it will affect what you can or will eat. Meat, hard cheeses, many fruits require that your dentition be intact and not pain causing. So get it taken care of - you need these food groups.

Gum disease left unattended or unseen by your dentist also can become a serious source of infection that can, and does seed not only to surgical implants but any organ of the body.

- **Regular Visits to your Oculist or Ophthalmologist**
  If you can't see trouble clearly, you can't avoid trouble. Your vision needs to be tested for changes that may be unappreciated by you, especially if they occur over time. You may think, ahh well it's a normal part of the aging process, and accept diminished vision - bad idea and not valid.

  Yes it can be true, that a visual problem is not entirely treatable (e.g. Macular degeneration etc.) but by and large this is not the case. Vision is often correctable, either by prescribed glasses or even surgery (e.g. cataracts.)

Normally speaking our vision does undergo a major change when we hit our 40s or 50's, and for the first time need glasses or contacts. This is so even if we have known problems of near sightedness or far sightedness, and have worn corrective lenses. But these optical conditions need to be current treatment- whether it's just a check of your vision, new glasses, or even surgery.

MDs and the medications they prescribe for you believe it or not are a Slip and Fall prevention tool. Even though it may not appear so immediately take my word as a physician, we can help with making you aware of how medications affect your stability, balance, and general overall condition.

JOURNAL

_____

_____

_____

_____

_____

_____

_____

_____

_____

_____

_____

_____

_____

CHAPTER 8
IT'S HAPPENED – I'VE FALLEN

- I've Fallen, Steps to Follow
- An Ounce of Prevention is worth a Pound of Cure

It's Happened - I've Fallen

Steps to Follow

Despite all preventative measures, falls do happen. So let's review what to do step-by-step.

I know that if you've fallen you may be shocked, upset or frightened, and clear thoughts about what to do can be difficult. Never the less, there are things that you can, and should do, as soon as you regain a little calm.

And the first thing to do is take a deep breath or even three, and quieten down as best you can, so enabling the next steps on your behalf.

STEP 1: Stop. Stay exactly where you've Fallen
Take another few breaths, then - get hold of either your medic alert bracelet or cell phone to notify and summon appropriate help. If you don't have these on your person

– if nothing else – yell and then, <u>yell some more</u>. When you're silent no one knows you've fallen.

STEP 2: Wait exactly where you are - Don't try to rise yet
Consider, you want someone to help. Do not be embarrassed by your fall and try to jump up or even or necessarily just plain get up.

STEP 3: Self-Check
Assess if and how you are Injured
You will sense whether or not you are badly hurt, and often whether you've broken a bone. A slight movement of each extremity will tell you all you need to know. What I'm talking about here is a very limited, informed self-test. A little motion of any extremity will tell you if you have trouble. Don't try to fix anything, just identify what's wrong.

Note: If you think you are badly injured, again, stay exactly where you are and await professional help which will be on its way!

Once you have ascertained that you are not seriously injured, and want and feel you can rise from the floor – here we go:

- **In your Home**
    1. Roll onto your side.
    2. Bend your knees up to your waist.
    3. Inch your way over to the nearest stable object (chair or bed).
    4. Reach up and grab onto it still on your side.

5. Scrunch right up close to the object.
6. Using your free hand as a push up and the chair in the other, try to roll over on to your knees.
7. If you succeed, now use both hands on the chair to get to a standing position, and as soon as possible turn and sit.
8. If you can't manage this, do not worry, simply stay where you are until help arrives.

- **Outdoors**
  1. Stay down.
  2. Above all do not let someone offer to raise you to your feet, until you have assessed your condition. Someone will probably have called an ambulance, which is a good idea.
  3. If you are offered a coat or jacket, accept.
  4. But If you think you can rise, use the nearest set of strong arms just as you would a chair. Then find the nearest place where you can sit and regain balance and calm.

- **Public Venue**
  1. In a theater, church or the like, if you can, regain your seat.
  2. Move each extremity lightly. But if any question - stay right where you are.
  3. The chances are someone in authority will have phoned 911.
  4. Let them come and assess you with good grace.
  5. And only then concern yourself with your final destination.

An Ounce of Prevention is Worth a Pound of Cure.

As we grow older much conspires to make us feel helpless - or at least not entirely in control of things as we were with our younger selves.

Reactions are not as quick, muscles not quite so powerful. And you can complete the rest of this thought. What it amounts to is a feeling that we are not as in control of our lives and activities as we may have been.

Fair is fair, this is not an imperceptive observation. But we sometimes surrender more than we need to. **Although we must acknowledge the physical phenomena of aging, what we sometimes fail to do is acknowledge the power of our minds, our insights into how things work, and our place within our physical world.**

If we allow or prepare intelligently, then the physical becomes much more manageable. That is precisely the point that I wished to make in this Slip and Fall prevention manual. It's a tool, even a weapon that you can use on your own behalf; to counter what in aging may have become hazardous.

I insist in the belief that it is entirely within the possible to teach old dog's new tricks - if the proffered reward is sufficiently tantalizing.

Here's another specific consideration that I've not yet covered in my text, but remains very much material for your personal daily life choices - the issue of diet and exercise.

What may be fine for the teeth and stomach of a twenty year old, may not be suitable or even do-able in its entirety for a much older person. There are many sources of information on what constitutes a balanced and healthy diet for our aging bodies. Find one and use it.

The same is true for exercise. It remains a key factor in health and conditioning, but the means of achieving and maintaining it will need modification to individual physical limitations of the older person.

Again, there are many specific and well qualified programs to be found in print and online. I will not iterate them here.

At any age, learning and mastering a new subject or even sport is as the kids say it, 'a blast!' And a new, helpful blast is just what is called for to lend a sense of self-confidence and even novelty often diminished as we age.

Such is Slip and Fall Prevention.

JOURNAL

_____

_____

_____

_____

_____

_____

_____

_____

_____

_____

_____

_____

_____

CHAPTER 9
LET'S TALK EXERCISE

9

First Things First

Before starting an exercise regime you should consult your doctor. Let him or her know you are going to begin exercising or increasing your activity level.

All exercises should be done next to a person, chair, or railing, that can be used for balance in case you become unsteady. Do not engage in exercises that seem overly challenging, unless you have been given the go-ahead by your doctor.

Doing a few gentle, at-home exercises regularly may help enhance your coordination and decrease the risk of falling. There are actually three types of exercise. Many may serve all three activities simultaneously. These are:

1. Aerobic, (for heart and lungs),
2. Isotonic (for flexibility) and
3. Isometric (for strength)

How Much, How Often?

Obviously it is good to do some of each type on a regular basis.

There are many, many ways to achieve each type. I will suggest only one Simple example of each. You will want to go on to develop your own regimen to suit your ability, circumstances, and keenness. What counts is that you develop your own program. And I think preferably AT HOME,

- Where daily work is easier and more convenient.
- In the setting where you can control Slip and Fall.
- Where keeping records of what you do, and any problems are simpler.

AEROBIC (For heart and lungs)

Knee Lifts

Knees ups or lifts are almost like a simulated marching in place.

Lift your knees as high as possible while holding on to a chair or table with one hand, simply march in place.

- Start for one minute, gradually increase time to 5 minutes. Increase the pace gradually to what you consider 'brisk' (you should pant a little as you perform).
- Work on it every other day.
- If you prefer you can do these as aqua exercises in a pool (it's the Cadillac of aerobics, and easily done). Just be sure you get to the pool regularly.

One good alternative is fast walking on an even, well-lit street or track.

- Start for 1 minute go and return.
- Increase your time gradually.
- A total of ½ hour is the eventual goal.

ISOMETRIC (Muscle strengthening)
These can be done entirely in a chair (for those of you who may have back problems.)

- As an orthopedist, I much prefer increasing repetitions at low weights to striving for large single weights. You are much more likely to avoid injury (strains & sprains) and you accomplish toning your muscles.

Especially important are exercising the large muscles in your thighs (the quads).

Leg Strengthening Exercises

Seated Leg Lift
- Sit in a sturdy chair with your back supported and simply straighten your leg before you.

- Breathe in and out slowly, extend one leg in front of you as straight as possible, but don't lock your knee.
- Flex foot-toes toward the ceiling. Hold for 1 second.
- Breathe in as you slowly lower leg back down.
- Repeat 10 to 15 times.
- Repeat 10 to 15 times with other leg.
- Repeat 10 to 15 more times with each leg.
- You can then add 1-2 pounds of weight (ankle weights or fill a stocking with a can of vegetables tied to it.)

ISOTONIC (flexibility)

These apply to every area of your body, but are absolutely straightforward in their most basic form.

Every extremity, your back and neck you put through a full range of motion. From flexion to extension.

- Arms Raises
- Ankle Circles
- Shoulder Stretch

I FIND IT HELPFUL TO DOUBLE CHECK FULL RANGE OF Motion by looking in the mirror. One thing to keep in mind - as you start all of the exercises including isotonic, don't be discouraged if you either can't do many reps or cannot do a full range of motion. Don't give up. Be patient with yourself. YOU WILL IMPROVE!!!

Your surgeon may want you supervised in a P.T. Facility. I think that supervised work has its merits, especially when you start. I find that more consistency is gained at home in the end.

However, most important - if you WORK WITH A PHYSICAL THERAPIST, OR TRAINER be sure they understand and accept that you cannot and should not perform things appropriate to a younger person. If you listen, your OWN BODY, will tell you what your limits are and I suggest strongly that you have the wisdom not to exceed them. The no pain, no gain is one of the most atrocious and harmful exercise mantras ever devised - and most especially for those over 55.

(Balance) The Three Point Stance

Balance in general while just standing or moving can become a real issue. It is a phenomenon we don't even think of in youth. However, with years the muscles of the back and thigh are perhaps not quite as strong and reliable as we would like. Unfortunately the resultant diminution of balance is the direct cause of many falls.

So… is that it? Is it an inevitable problem? I don't think so, but here is a specific counter that will really modify if not prevent the balancing problem. It's called a three point stance.

It is the most consistent and balanced standing position you can adapt, especially if you use it consistently, when rising from a seated position, or while standing for any length of time. You will probably have to work on it, but if it becomes a habit, you will be pleased at the consistent steadiness it produces.

I described this earlier in the book, but think it so important I risk re-iteration.

3 point stance - Illustration

- One foot is turned to the side and one foot points straight forward. (For righties, it's most effective if the right foot is the forward one, for lefties it's the left that should be forward).

Now the three point stance deals with a balanced posture. But we can do more than that. We can actively work on our ability to balance when in motion.

Round The Table Balancing

Stand at your kitchen or dining room table having first cleared the chairs around it.

Then step close extend both arms straight and move in crabwise steps around its circumference. Once in a clockwise direction, once in a counter-clock wise.

Work up gradually to six reps.

When you can do this steadily and without undue fatigue, Do the exercise using one hand.

Work up to six reps.

Now try it without supporting hands, using one hand only if you NEED it.

JOURNAL

_____

_____

_____

_____

_____

_____

_____

_____

_____

_____

_____

_____

_____

_____

CHAPTER 10
A FINAL WORD

10

I can't resist having the final word. Your safety in all circumstances starts and ends with "Staying in the Moment"! It will allow you to manage your surroundings and the hazards they may present.

What is meant by staying in the moment has been expressed in many ways - many if not all will be familiar to you.

For example, don't try to throw a ball before you've caught it, keep focus on what is right before you, do one thing at a time. Daydreaming is great, but not until you've reached a safe perch.

Distraction is invariably the serious enemy of safe and sound, and to be avoided at all moments. I could go on, but I think you get the notion and its importance.

One final thought, our personal independence as we age depends of being aware of, and to the greatest extent possible controlling our space or surroundings.

So a toast….**Here's to us old dogs learning new tricks…here's to self-help…and here's to preventing Slip and Falls!**

Disclaimer

Note to the reader. This book contains informational material and opinions. It is sold and distributed with the understanding that the publisher and author do not intend to render any kind of medical or surgical services. The opinions expressed are those of the author, and are not to be construed as anything other than opinion.

M.E. Hecht, M.D.
Orthopedic Surgeon I Author I Columnist

M.E. Hecht, M.D., is a published author, freelance writer and Orthopedic Surgeon; she writes both fiction and nonfiction. She first entered the business world to fuel her passion for medicine and writing, and continues to fulfill this passion today with published works for Vogue Magazine, Sunrise River Press, The Wall Street Journal, American Medical News, Medical Tribune, and others.

Born in Baltimore Maryland and scion of the Hecht family department store chain in Baltimore, she attended New York University and Johns Hopkins College receiving her BA in English Literature. Continuing with her love and prowess of the arts she was invited to attend Yale Universities Drama School.

At the age of 33, she decided to change careers and attend Medical School. She was accepted to Columbia University for Pre-med and then received her M.D. from the State University of New York (SUNY).

She did her residency training in surgery and orthopedics at Long Island Jewish Hospital Center and was then awarded clinical instructor of Orthopedics at Mount Sinai School of Medicine. Dr. Hecht went on to become the Assistant Chief of Orthopedics at Elmhurst Hospital an affiliate of Mount Sinai School of Medicine. Believing in the importance of patient education and prior to private practice, Dr. Hecht established the Country's First Organization for Second Opinions prior to Elective Surgery. She continued to teach and practice orthopedic surgery until her retirement in 1998.

Made in the USA
Columbia, SC
06 November 2019